Be the Change! Shaping Your Community

Be a COMMUNITY LEADER!

By Kristen Rajczak Nelson

Gareth Stevens
PUBLISHING

Please visit our website, www.garethstevens.com. For a free color catalog of all our high-quality books, call toll free 1-800-542-2595 or fax 1-877-542-2596.

Library of Congress Cataloging-in-Publication Data

Names: Rajczak Nelson, Kristen, author.
Title: Be a community leader! / Kristen Rajczak Nelson.
Description: New York : Gareth Stevens Publishing, [2019] | Series: Be the change! Shaping your community | Includes index.
Identifiers: LCCN 2017046107| ISBN 9781538219997 (library bound) | ISBN 9781538220016 (pbk.) | ISBN 9781538220023 (6 pack)
Subjects: LCSH: Civic leaders. | Leadership–Psychological aspects.
Classification: LCC HN42 .R35 2018 | DDC 303.3/4–dc23
LC record available at https://lccn.loc.gov/2017046107

First Edition

Published in 2019 by
Gareth Stevens Publishing
111 East 14th Street, Suite 349
New York, NY 10003

Copyright © 2019 Gareth Stevens Publishing

Designer: Laura Bowen
Editor: Joan Stoltman

Photo credits: Cover, p. 1 (main) Maskot/Getty Images; cover, p. 1 (background) KidStock/Blend Images/Getty Images; p. 4 Sergey Novikov/Shutterstock.com; pp. 5, 9 Hero Images/Getty Images; pp. 6-7 Bloomberg/Getty Images; p. 11 fstop123/E+/Getty Images; p. 12 Dmytro Zinkevych/Shutterstuck.com; p. 13 kali9/E+/Getty Images; p. 15 asiseeit/E+/Getty Images; p. 17 gchutka/E+/Getty Images; p. 19 Alistair Berg/Iconica/Getty Images; p. 20 Thomas Barwick/Iconica/Getty Images; p. 21 Annabelle Breakey/Taxi/Getty Images; p. 22 J. Countess/Getty Images Entertainment/Getty Images; p. 23 CBS Photo Archive/CBS/Getty Images; pp. 24-25 Africa Studio/Shutterstock.com; p. 27 ER_09/Shutterstock.com; p. 28 Joseph Sohm/Shutterstock.com; p. 29 MANDY GODBEHEAR/Shutterstock.com.

Printed in the United States of America

CPSIA compliance information: Batch #CS18GS: For further information contact Gareth Stevens, New York, New York at 1-800-542-2595.

CONTENTS

Words in the glossary appear in **bold** type the first time they are used in the text.

Leaders All Around You

Do you look up to someone in your life? Your dad, a teacher, and an older cousin are all great answers. What about people in your community? From the fire chief to your youth group leader, there are so many leaders in your communities whom you could look up to and learn from.

Community leaders don't have to be adults, though! In fact, you can be a leader in your community if you want! Being a community leader is a great experience that can help you learn more about yourself, where you live, and even about the political process!

What is a community?

Communities are simply groups of people that have something in common, like where they live, what they do for fun, or what they care about. Communities can be just a few people or a group of thousands! Your soccer team is a community. Your school and town are, too!

Who Are Community Leaders?

Community leaders are those who take on the responsibility of heading a group. They often want to make their community better and believe they could help do that. Some community leaders have special skills relating to a group, such as a former **competitive** runner who coaches a local running group or a **professional** actor who directs a play at a community theater.

Your Turn!

If you see a place where you can take on certain responsibilities to make your community better, you can be a community leader right now! Does your acting club need someone to organize the costumes for an upcoming play? Does your youth group need someone to talk to new kids about joining?

Community leaders often step into their position because they want to make sure whatever needs to be done will get done. They often care a lot about what their community is doing right now and about the future of that community.

Did you know that you're already a member of several communities? At the very least, you're a member of your town, state, and country community, as well as the world community. Leaders of the world community work together as United Nations **delegates** to get things done!

President Trump speaking at a United Nations meeting

7

What's in a Name?

Some community leaders have official positions. They might even have titles like "**volunteer** organizer," "coach," "scout leader," or "president." However, there are many more community leaders than just those with official positions. That's because any person who takes responsibility for part of making a community run better is a leader.

From the teacher who always organizes the school bake sale to the girl in your class who takes the notes for your group project, community leaders aren't always recognized. But their contributions to a community are just as important as the principal or official group leader.

Supporting the Leader

In most communities, there's too much for just one person to do. People can be community leaders by supporting the official leaders of a group. Stepping up to take on small jobs, such as making an event poster, shows leadership and helps your community meet its goals. Every task builds toward success!

Qualities of Great Leaders

Being an effective leader takes many kinds of skills. Leaders often have to spend more time working on projects, ideas, and organization than others. Community leaders have to be both hard workers and smart workers because they may have a lot to do in a short time!

Sometimes being a smart leader means asking for help. Great leaders understand teamwork. They don't try to do everything themselves. Leaders spend time figuring out who in their community would be the best for a job and ask them for help. Called delegating, this is the best way to get tasks done faster and better!

Problems

Leaders of all communities need to be good at problem solving. People in the community who have a problem will turn to a leader for the answer. Leaders need to be ready to listen, calmly make a decision, and encourage **compromise** and teamwork throughout the process of problem solving.

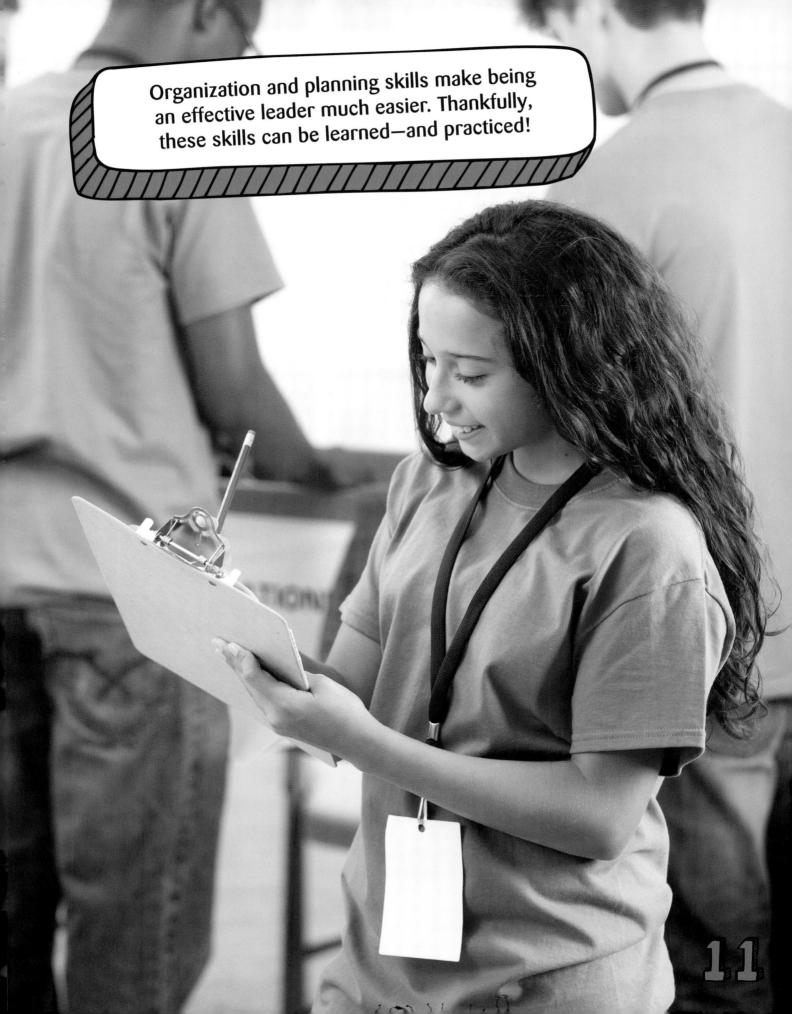

Another important leadership skill is being able to communicate well, including through email, on the phone, in text messages, when talking to a few people, and when speaking to a big group. Leaders think before they speak. They're also great listeners because they know that other people have valuable ideas that should be heard and considered.

In listening to others, great community leaders may find they need to know more about a subject, such as the city's recycling program. They're willing to ask questions and seek out knowledgeable people to learn more, adapting to whatever problems they face!

Dream Big!

Great leaders come up with big goals for their community, as well as plan smaller steps to meet these goals! To make a community **environmentally** friendly, for example, planning recycling programs, bicycle-sharing programs, and requesting that laws be changed are some of the ways to get that big idea accomplished!

Become a Better Leader

There are many steps you can take to work on your leadership skills now! You can start by seeing if your school, library, or local community center offers classes in leadership skills. Classes, groups, or clubs that give you the chance to learn public speaking are especially helpful to find!

You can spend time working on your communication skills without taking any special classes. If you're not sure about talking to others, practice by calling to make your own appointments. Ask your friends or family to have **debates** with you so you can practice giving your opinion clearly.

Your Turn!

One great way to learn about leadership is to observe a leader you respect. This can be a public figure or someone you know. If it's someone you know, ask them to become your **mentor**. You can talk to them about what they like and don't like about being a leader and how they overcome problems.

Your mentor may suggest ways you can become a better leader, such as being captain of your swim team or working in your school's student government.

Make a Difference!

Community leaders keep towns, schools, and groups running. Without them taking charge, it's unlikely some communities would even stay together! Would your book club meet if the leader never set up a time and place to get together?

Community leaders have the chance to really make a difference in the world around them. When a local librarian runs a book drive for a school with little money, the students at that school gain a chance to read and learn more. If your class president organizes a performance by the school band to celebrate the end of the school year, many people have a chance to enjoy that music!

Your Turn!

Start working toward goals now so you have plenty of practice in accomplishing them. First, pick a goal. Next, break it down into smaller pieces that can be completed along the way. Finally, write down the ways you're going to work toward each piece of your goal every day.

Many people become community leaders because they really want to do things for their community. They have ideas ranging from raising money for a good cause to bringing a popular athlete to town to speak.

The Path to Leadership

In smaller communities, many leaders take on their position simply because they want to. They notice something that needs doing and they decide to take on the responsibility. In most cases, there aren't any rules about being a community leader! Someone who cares about trash building up in a park can simply call some friends and work to clean it up one Saturday morning.

But community members can also become leaders in more official ways. The same concerned park lover could go speak at a town meeting about the park—or even apply for a job at the parks department if they're old enough!

More Voices

The more leaders there are, the more voices can be heard. All communities need **diversity** in their leadership. There's a lot to be learned from **minority groups**, women, younger people, and those with disabilities. They can bring in points of view the community should consider!

Some people are happy to quietly lead small groups within their community. Others want to make changes on a larger scale and use the government or businesses to meet their goals.

Run for Office!

Some of the most visible community leaders are political or government leaders, such as mayors, state representatives, and members of Congress. People in their communities often come to them with problems that are too hard for citizens to solve on their own. Politicians often have money and a team of people behind them to help address these problems.

Community leaders in positions of power, such as the mayor, can **focus** their efforts by listening to their community to learn what people think needs to be done. Once they find out what's most important to the most people, they can begin work on that first!

Your Turn!

Becoming a member of your school's student government is a great way to be a community leader. You'll hear the concerns of other students and try to address them. Can you throw a pizza party for the winning soccer team? Would you be able to change the date of the school talent show?

COMMUNITY LEADERS IN GOVERNMENT

MAYOR
leads a village, town, or city

STATE SENATOR/ STATE REPRESENTATIVE
represents a part of a state in the state government

MEMBER OF HOUSE OF REPRESENTATIVES
represents a part of a state in Congress

GOVERNOR
leads a state

US SENATOR
represents a state in Congress

Community leaders working in politics and the government try to pass laws—or make changes to laws—to make a difference!

Act Now!

Another important way you can be a community leader is to be an activist. Activists are people who feel very strongly about a cause, such as world hunger, voters' rights, or **climate change**. They want changes to happen in their town, state, country, or sometimes even the whole world!

Activists often form groups so they can more effectively plan meetings, marches, or other events to get their message out to the public. The Women's Marches that took place all over the United States in January 2017 are an example of community leadership by activists.

Activists can be anyone, including celebrities. Actress Emma Watson spoke at the United Nations in 2014 about equality for all sexes.

A Brave Young Girl

Activists can be any age! Malala Yousafzai was just 11 years old when she started writing about a law that stopped girls from going to school in her country, Pakistan. She was shot for speaking out—but even that didn't stop her. She still speaks out today about the right to education for girls.

☆★☆★☆★☆★☆★

Giving Time

Many times, community leaders are volunteers and don't make money for their position. They often have other full-time jobs and do their work as a leader outside of the work they're paid for. They might even do enough work that their community leadership takes up the same amount of time as their everyday job!

Your Turn!

Volunteering within your community can make a real difference today. Plan a time for your friends to volunteer at a soup kitchen together. Organize a group of classmates to read to younger kids at school. You'll love the way you feel afterward—and you've done some good in your world!

Community leaders often feel like they're "paid" in other ways, however. They see their community grow, their message reach more people, and changes happen in other people's lives. To see your efforts making a difference may be a greater reward than money ever could be!

A great way to give back and practice your leadership skills is to start a volunteering club at your school!

DONATIONS

Start Here!

Are you ready to be a community leader? Here are some questions to ask yourself to find out:

- What communities am I a part of? Are there communities I want to become active in?

- What would I like to change or make better about one of my communities?

- What would need to be done to make that change happen?

- Do I have the skills to meet the goals that would bring about change?

Committing to a cause can be scary at first because you don't know exactly what's ahead of you. Once you get started, however, you'll find it's exciting!

Your Turn!

Community leadership positions can help you when you apply to special high schools, colleges, or even jobs. They prove to possible future bosses and schools that you have what it takes to work hard and meet goals. Plus, many of the skills you need for community leadership carry over into the working world!

If you still aren't sure about stepping into a leadership **role**, start small. Collect field trip money for the science club, or help some of your neighbors with their lawn or with getting their trash and recycling to the curb.

One of the keys to making sure you enjoy your community leadership role is to work on something you love. Whether that's being in Boy Scouts or Girl Scouts, being the head volunteer at the local animal shelter, or directing the student play, leadership is most rewarding when you care about what you're doing.

The work of a community leader is never done, but you should always take some time to enjoy the best part of the job—your community! People, not events or goals, make a community great. Community leaders just help make them a little better!

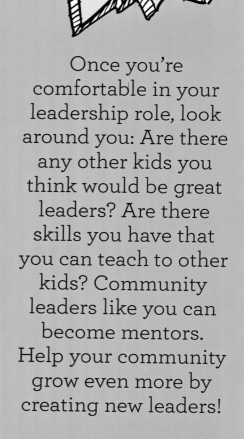

Your Turn!

Once you're comfortable in your leadership role, look around you: Are there any other kids you think would be great leaders? Are there skills you have that you can teach to other kids? Community leaders like you can become mentors. Help your community grow even more by creating new leaders!

LEAD YOUR COMMUNITY!

Gather a group to visit a nursing home!

Run for class president!

Start a recycling club at school!

Be the head cheerleader!

Volunteer to be in charge of collecting class gifts!

Do the morning announcements at school!

Being a community leader is hard work, but don't forget to have fun with it! The people around you will be excited about the same things you are, so new friendships are sure to grow!

GLOSSARY

climate change: long-term change in Earth's climate, caused partly by human activities such as burning oil and natural gas

competitive: having to do with an event in which people try to beat others

compromise: a way of two sides reaching agreement in which each gives up something to end an argument

debate: an argument or public discussion

delegate: a person who is chosen or elected to vote or act for others

diversity: the state of having many different kinds, especially races, ethnicities, and genders

environmental: having to do with the natural world in which a plant or animal lives

focus: to direct your attention or effort at something specific

mentor: someone who provides advice and support to a less experienced person

minority group: people who are not part of the main group of a society. In the United States, African Americans, Native Americans, Latinos, and the poor are minority groups.

motivate: to increase someone's interest in doing something

professional: earning money from an activity that many people do for fun

role: a function performed by someone in a certain situation

volunteer: a person who works without being paid. Also, to work without pay.

FOR MORE INFORMATION

BOOKS

James, Emily. *How to Be a Good Citizen: A Question and Answer Book About Citizenship.* North Mankato, MN: Capstone Press, 2018.

Peters, Elisa. *Malala Yousafzai: Pakistani Activist for Female Education.* New York, NY: Rosen Publishing Group, 2018.

Wooster, Patricia. *So, You Want to Be a Leader? An Awesome Guide to Becoming a Head Honcho.* New York, NY: Aladdin, 2016.

WEBSITES

Congress for Kids: Citizenship
www.congressforkids.net/citizenship_1_whatis.htm
Find out more about what it means to be a US citizen and part of the national community.

Counties Work
www.icivics.org/games/counties-work
Play a game in which you'll try to solve problems as a county official would!

Publisher's note to educators and parents: Our editors have carefully reviewed these websites to ensure that they are suitable for students. Many websites change frequently, however, and we cannot guarantee that a site's future contents will continue to meet our high standards of quality and educational value. Be advised that students should be closely supervised whenever they access the internet.

INDEX